IMAGES OF WAR

THE RISE OF HITLER

RARE PHOTOGRAPHS FROM WARTIME ARCHIVES

Translated by
TREVOR SALISBURY

Pen & Sword
MILITARY

First published in Great Britain in 2015 by
PEN & SWORD MILITARY
an imprint of
Pen & Sword Books Ltd,
47 Church Street, Barnsley,
South Yorkshire.
S70 2AS

ISBN 978 1 47382 218 4

A CIP catalogue record for this book is available
from the British Library

Designed by Faction Press
Printed and bound in Malta by Gutenberg Press Ltd

Pen & Sword Books Ltd incorporates the imprints of Aviation, Atlas,
Family History, Fiction, Maritime, Military, Discovery, Politics, History,
Archaeology, Select, Wharncliffe Local History, Wharncliffe True Crime,
Military Classics, Wharncliffe Transport, Leo Cooper, The Praetorian Press,
Remember When, Seaforth Publishing and Frontline Publishing.

For a complete list of Pen & Sword titles please contact:
PEN & SWORD BOOKS LIMITED
47 Church Street, Barnsley, South Yorkshire, S70 2AS, England.
E-mail: enquiries@pen-and-sword.co.uk
Website: www.pen-and-sword.co.uk

Contents

Introduction

This book that I was asked to translate and annotate concerns a man who, despite his unbounded evilness, was able to assert limitless power over a nation before creating maximum of misery for millions. I can only assume that the millions of his countrymen wholeheartedly wished to believed his promises and like sheep they followed his every word and believed everything he said with all their hearts and thus the scene was set for total disaster.

The original book upon which this is based was found in the ruins of a bombed-out house in one of Germany's ruined cities, it being divest of its cover and all the worse for wear. The tattered book *Deutschland Erwache* came to England by way of a British soldier who brought it home as a souvenir. Some of the pages had suffered water damage so that an effort had to be made to try and salvage some of the illustrations. The supporting photographs come from the Taylor Archives so as to fill out the story of *The Rise of Hitler*. The account is based upon this spoiled book of propaganda (and that is certainly what it is) set in a period of history, the events of which should never be repeated.

The captions are in different fonts so as to set the original text, the translation and added captions apart. I believe that the original book is typical of the propaganda of the time with the obvious non-critical acceptance of everything that Adolf Hitler was and what he stood for. The original book attempted to present him as a peace-loving man who wanted nothing other than peace and quiet in his 'beloved Alps' and who dearly loved children and was kind to all. But as we all know, the truth was completely different. When looking through the photographs, it is very striking that one only sees him accompanied by those of his own kind. No attempt was made to try and even pretend that he had contact with others that thought differently.

But who exactly was Baldur von Shirach, the author of the 1930s book?

Shirach was born 9 May 1907 in Berlin and interestingly enough, his mother was in fact an American. (It would have been interesting to know what she thought of his infatuation with Hitler later.)

His first contact with Hitler came at the age of eighteen, when he met him at his parents' home. It must have so impressed him that he joined the National Socialist party shortly afterwards. Upon discontinuing his studies at the University of Munich, he became the leader of the National Socialist Student Association (NSDStB) in 1928. The next step up the Nazi hierarchy ladder followed three years later with his appointment as Reich Youth Leader in the NSDAP – and a high position in the SA accompanied that promotion.

One year later he became the son-in-law of Heinrich Hoffmann, the photographer he pretends is just a press photographer being a nuisance to the Führer. After he married Hoffmann's daughter, Henriette, in the same year (1932), he was elected to the Reichstag. When the Nazis came to power one year later, he assumed responsibility for the entire extra school education of youngsters in the new Reich and that was also the year in which he started publishing his propaganda books in cooperation with his father-in-law Heinrich Hoffmann.

Further political advancements in his career were State Secretary in 1936 and his voluntary war service in 1939, for which he was awarded the Iron Cross, Second Class. His most despicable action occurred commencing in 1941, when he was responsible for deporting the Jews from Vienna. However, in 1943, he appears to have thought better of it because he demanded that the East Europeans be treated better and after his wife criticised Hitler for the deportations, he was no long looked upon favourably by Hitler.

In 1945, Shirach was brought before the military tribunal in Nuremberg and was sentenced to twenty years imprisonment which he served in Berlin-Spandau prison. He died in 1974.

Baldur von Shirach before the military tribunal at Nuremberg; to his right seated is Joachim von Ribbentrop, who would be hung for his crimes.

Hitler's rise to absolute power is a phenomenon of the modern age.

Das ist an ihm das Größte: daß er nicht
nur unser Führer ist und vieler Held,
sondern er selber: Grade, fest und schlicht.

Daß in ihm ruhn die Wurzeln unsrer Welt
und seine Seele an die Sterne Strich
und er doch Mensch blieb, so wie du und ich.

That is the greatest thing about him: that he is not
only our Führer and a hero for many
but he is himself: honest, steadfast and modest.

That the roots of our world rest within him
and his soul brushed against the stars
and he nevertheless remained one of us.

BALDUR VON SHIRACH: ZUM GELEIT

Wem das Glück zuteil wurde, zu dem Führer des jungen Deutschland als Mitarbeiter in ein engeres Vertrauensverhältnis zu treten, der wurde und wird immer wieder gepackt und ergriffen von jener der Öffentlichkeit nicht zugewandten Wesensseite Adolf Hitlers, die mit dem vorliegenden Buch auch dem weiteren Kreise seiner Freunde zugänglich gemacht werden soll.

Was Adolf Hitler, der Führer, für sein Volk bedeutet, wird heute von Millionen gewußt oder gefühlt. Diesem Fühlen und Wissen Gestalt zu geben, wird Aufgabe der Geschichtsschreibung sein, die den historischen Hitler den Enkeln zu überliefern hat. Das Buch über den Führer wird somit erst in einer ferneren Zeit geschrieben werden können, die mit dem größeren Abstand zugleich die größere Urteilskraft erlangt haben wird.
Hier geht es um anderes.

Der Deutsche verlangt mit Recht (denn dies entspricht seinem Wesen und inneren Gesetz), daß der von ihm erkorene Führer gewissermaßen eine Synthese aus Werk und Persönlichkeit darstelle. Er fordert darüber hinaus von seinem Führer auch in den privaten Dingen des Lebens Vorbildlichkeit und menschliche Größe. So erklären sich die Liebe und Verehrung, die unser Volk zwei größten Söhnen, Goethe und Friedrich dem Großen, entgegenbringt, so erklärt sich aber auch jener fanatische Glaube an Adolf Hitler, für den täglich Nationalsozialisten verwundet und ermordet werden, für den wir alle in Gefahr und Gefängnis gegangen sind.

Baldur Benedikt von Schirach was a Nazi youth leader later convicted of crimes against humanity. He was the head of the Hitler-Jugend (Hitler Youth') and later Gauleiter and *Reichsstatthalter* (Reich Governor) of Vienna.

BALDUR VON SHIRACH: TRIBUTE

Baldur Benedikt von Schirach (9 May 1907 – 8 August 1974)

Those who are lucky enough to be in a close relationship of trust with the Führer of the young Germany, will and always shall be packed and seized by a part of Adolf Hitler´s nature that the public does not see, but which should be disclosed to the wide circle of his friends with this book.

Today, millions of people know or feel what Adolf Hitler, the Führer, means to his people. The giving of this feeling and knowledge of a form will be the task belying the writing of the story of the Hitler of the past that can be told to the grandchildren. The book about the Führer can therefore only be written some time in the future as the power of judgement shall increase in strength, the more time has passed

.

This concerns itself with something else.
The German is right in demanding (in keeping with his nature and the inner law of his being), that the Führer he elects should be a certain synthesis between work and personality. He also demands that his Führer also sets an example and has an upstanding character in his private life. This not only explains the love and veneration our people feels for two of its greatest sons, Goethe and Friedrich the Great, but also its fanatic belief in Adolf Hitler, for whom National Socialists are killed and wounded every day and for whom we are all we were in danger and imprisoned.

Zwei Eigenschaften möchte ich als die mir augen-
fälligsten Züge im Wesen Adolf Hitlers bezeichnen:
Kraft und Güte. Es sind zugleich die Eigenschaften,
die in den Bildern dieses Buches deutlich werden.
Ob Hitler im Kraftwagen durch Deutschland fährt
und umbraust wird vom jubelnden Zuruf der
Straßenarbeiter, ob er aufgewühlt und erschüttert
am Lager eines ermordeten Kameraden steht,
immer ist um ihn diese Hoheit und tiefste
Menschlichkeit, die so oft denen, die ihm zum
erstenmal entgegentreten, die Rede verschlägt, ob
sie nun Jünglinge, gereifte Männer oder Greise
sind. Möge dieses Buch, das fast durchweg
unbekannte und unveröffentlichte Abbildungen per-
sönlicher Erlebnisse Adolf Hitlers wiedergibt, weit
über die Kreise der nationalsozialistischen
Bewegung hinaus den Eindruck vermitteln helfen,
den wir empfangen haben, die wir jahrelang unter
ihm arbeiten durften und ihn dabei verehren und

Photograph of the Führer around 1921.

lieben lernten. Heute liegt der Schatten dieses Mannes über Deutschland, und fas-
sungslos staunen viele über das Wunder, daß nach absoluter Herrschaft des
Marxismus ein Einziger das Antlitz der Nation so zu wandeln vermochte.

*Two of the most obvious aspects of Adolf Hitler´s character are strength and
kindness. These are also the aspects that are made clear in this book. No matter
whether he is travelling through Germany in a car to the roaring jubilation of
road workers, whether he is standing next to the bed of a murdered comrade,
shaken inside and shocked, it is always this grandeur and deepest humanity,
that takes the breath away from those that meet him for the first time, whether
a young boy, an adult man or an old one. May this book that includes
photographs depicting the personal experiences of Adolf Hitler, many of which
being unknown and never having been published before, help to give the
impression that we, who have had the privilege of being able to work with him
for many years and in doing so, have come to worship and love him, have
gained to all those far outside the National Socialist movement. The shadow of
this man has now cast itself over Germany and many are speechless at the
wonder that comes that a single person has succeeded in changing the face of
the nation so radically after the end of the Marxist autocracy.*

Wer diese Bilder als Bekenntnisse mit offenem Herzen liest, der ahnt vielleicht das
Geheimnis dieser einzigartigen Persönlichkeit. Und begreift: Hier offenbart sich

nicht allein ein mitreißender Führer, sondern ein großer und guter Mensch.
Populär sein heißt: viel photographiert werden. Adolf Hitler hat sich immer dagegen gesträubt, Objekt der Photographen zu sein. Besonders vor zwölf Jahren, als sein Name zum erstenmal aus dem Dunkel der Unbekanntheit auftauchte, war er ein erklärter Gegner der Kamera. Schon damals versuchte die illustrierte Presse der ganzen Welt ein Bild des Führers zu erlangen. Ohne Erfolg. Trotz hohe Geldangebote lehnte Hitler jede Bitte um Überlassung einer Aufnahme zum Zweck der Reproduktion rundweg ab.
Ein großes Witzblatt brachte damals unter der Überschrift „Wie sieht Hitler aus?" eine Reihe Karikaturen mit den unmöglichsten „Vorschlägen", wie man sich Hitler vorzustellen habe. Diese Tatsache illustriert den Zustand: man redete von Hitler, man lobte oder tadelte ihn – aber man wußte nich, wie er aussah.
In jener Zeit forderte eine große amerikanische Zeitung den Münchener Presse-Photographen Heinrich Hoffman auf, ihr ein Bild des Vorsitzenden der Nationalsozialistischen Deutschen Arbeiterpartei zu besorgen. Durch seinen Freund Dietrich Eckart versuchte Hoffmann nun eine günstige Gelegenheit für die Aufnahme zu erhalten.

Those who see these photographs as being confessions with an open heart, shall probably have an idea of the secret behind this unique personality and understand that this is not only the revelation of a rousing Führer, but also one of a great and good human being.
Being popular means having your photograph taken frequently. Adolf Hitler always tried to avoid having his photograph taken. He was especially a declared opponent of the camera twelve years ago, when his name emerged from the darkness of anonymity for the first time. It was already the case then that the international illustrated press tried to get a photograph of the Führer but without success. Hitler categorically refused to provide them with a photograph for reproduction purposes, despite him being offered large amounts of money.
A popular satirical magazine published a series of caricatures at the time with the most outrageous 'suggestions' under the heading 'What does Hitler look like?' This fact just went to prove the situation that one spoke of Hitler, one praised or rebuked him – but nobody knew what he looked like.
At that time, a large American newspaper requested the press photographer Heinrich Hoffmann from Munich to obtain a photograph of the Chairman of the National Socialist Workers´ Party (NSDAP). Hoffmann now hoped to find a good opportunity to take a photograph through his friend Dietrich Eckart.
Aber der Anschlag mißglückte. Zwar bekam Hoffmann den Führer zu sehen, als er im Begriff war, sein Auto zu besteigen, aber im Augenblick, wie er ihn photogra-

phieren wollte, stürzten drei hünenhafte Begleiter Hitlers auf ihn zu und hielten ihn fest, während der Wagen des Fahrers davonbrauste. Später hatte Hoffman mehr Glück: es gelang ihm, eine Aufnahme herzustellen, aber Hitler bat ihn, sie nicht zu veröffentlichen. Hoffmann folgte dem Wunsch des Führers, und aus Dank übertrug ihm später als seine Anhänger ihn nach Aufnahmen drängten, das alleinige Recht zur Herstellung seine Bilder für die nationalsozialistische Bewegung. Bald erkannte der Führer den ungeheueren propagandistischen Wert der Photographie für die nationalsozialistische Bewegung: während die Gazetten von der „Riesenpleite" nationalsozialistischer Versammlungen faselten, stellte Hoffmann seine

Heinrich Hoffmann, photographer, best known for his published photographs of Adolf Hitler.

Panoramabilder der großen Hitlerversammlungen her und widerlegte durch die Photographie die Lüge der Feinde. Das herzliche Freundschaftsverhältnis zwischen Adolf Hitler und seinem alten Mitkämpfer Hoffmann, der bald sein ständiger Reisebegleiter wurde, gab Hoffmann die Möglichkeit, Aufnahmen zu machen, wie sie eben nur einer herstellen kann, der in der engsten Umgebung des Führers weilt.

The attack was unsuccessful however. Hoffmann saw the Führer when he was about to get into his car but just when he was about to take the photograph, three of Hitler's huge bodyguards rushed up to him and held onto him whilst the driver sped off. Hoffmann had more luck later: he succeeded in taking a photograph but Hitler asked him not to publish it. He acted in accordance with the Führer's wishes and the Führer repaid him by granting him sole rights in the taking of pictures for the National Socialist movement when Hitler's supporters urged him to give them photographs later. The Führer soon recognised the propaganda value of photography for the National Socialist movement: whilst the newspapers were rambling on about the 'absolute disaster' of National Socialist conferences, Hoffmann was taking panoramic views of the largest Hitler conferences, thereby refuting the lies that were being told by the opposers. The cordial friendly relationship between Adolf Hitler and his former fellow combatant Hoffmann, who was soon to be his permanent travel companion, provided Hoffmann with the possibility of him being able to take photographs that could only be taken by someone who is as close to the Führer as possible.

Hierin liegt auch der eigentliche Reiz des vorliegenden Buches, dessen Aufgabe nicht in einer literarischen Darstellung des Lebens des Führers besteht, sondern in der unmittelbaren Wiedergabe eines tatsächlichen Gesehenen.

Hitler ist ein Universaler Geist. Es ist unmöglich, der Mannigfaltigkeit seines Wesens mit 100 Aufnahmen, die aus Tausenden ausgesucht wurden, gerecht zu werden. Es sollen hier nur einige Andeutungen über diese einmalige Persönlichkeit gemacht werden. Es ist fast unbekannt, daß Hitler Antialkoholiker, Nichtraucher und Vegetarier ist. Ohne andre – auch seine nächste Umgebung – im geringsten in dieser Richtung zu bevormunden, hält er sich eisern an das selbstauferlegte Lebensgesetz. Seine Arbeitsleistung ist ungeheuer. Nicht allein, daß er den Riesenapparat der nationalsozialistischen Bewegung leitet, er erträgt als Redner die anstrengenden Reisen, ist heute in Königsberg, morgen in Berlin, übermorgen in München, alles dies bei einem Minimum von Schlaf, denn der Führer arbeitet meist bis in die frühen Morgenstunden.

Über seine private Liebhabereien ist soviel geklatscht und gelogen worden, daß auch hierüber ein Wort gesagt werden muß. Seine größte Freude ist seine Bibliothek, die etwa 6000 Bände umfaßt, die er alle nicht nur durchblättert, sondern auch gelesen hat. Am stärksten sind in dieser Bücherei Architektur und Geschichte vertreten.

This is the real appeal of this book, the idea not being a literary description of the Führer's life, but in the direct reporting on what really did happen.

Hitler is a universal spirit. It is impossible to do justice to the diversity of his character with 100 photographs that have been selected from thousands. The aim here is to merely hint at a unique personality. It is almost an unknown fact that Hitler is a teetotaller, a non-smoker and a vegetarian. He displays iron discipline when adhering to his self-imposed law of life, without patronizing others – including those closest to him – even in the slightest. His work effort is unbelievable. Not only that he heads the enormous National Socialist movement apparatus alone, he also copes with the exhausting journeys as a speaker, he is in Königsberg today, in Berlin tomorrow and in Munich the day after; and all of this with a minimum amount of sleep, as the Führer normally works until the early hours of the morning.

There has been so much gossip and lies told about his hobbies, that they also have to be mentioned here. His greatest pleasure is his library that has around 6000 volumes, which he has not only leafed through; he has also read them all. Most of the books in this library are on the subjects of architecture and history.

Auch auf diesen beiden Gebieten ist Hitler eine unangreifbare Autorität. Kunst ist ihm Lebensbedürfnis, vor allem Musik; sein Wort: „Wenn die Künstler ahnen würden, was ich für die deutsche Kunst tun werde, hätte ich unter ihnen keinen Gegner" kennzeichnet die tiefe Absicht zu kultureller Tat. Naive Menschen meinen, Adolf Hitler führe ein Leben in Sorglosigkeit und Ruhe, mit Achtstundentag und Cafébesuch. Von der ganzen Schwere der Bürde, die auf den Schultern dieses Mannes ruht, ahnen die Wenigsten etwas.

Unsere Zeit wird diesen Überragenden vielleicht verehren und lieben, aber sie wird ihn nicht in seiner großen Tiefe ermessen können. Das braucht sie auch nicht. Sie soll nur immer wieder im Hinschauen auf die gewaltige Persönlichkeit des Führers ehrfürchtig werden und Gott im Himmel danken, daß er uns auch dieses Mal nicht verlassen hat.

Hitler knows more about these subjects than any other. The arts are a way of life to him, especially music; to express it in his own words: 'If the artists were aware of everything that I would do for German art then I would not have any of them as opponents.' This shows his far-reaching intention to become culturally active. Naive people claim that Adolf Hitler leads a life without cares and in rest, with an eight-hour day and with visits to cafés. There are few that have an idea of the weight of the burden that rests on the shoulders of this man. The people of our time will possibly worship and love this pre-eminence, but they will be unable to judge him in all his great depth. They do not need to. They should only occasionally look up towards heaven in awe and, in view of the Führer´s gigantic personality, thank the Lord that he still remains with us.

Nürnberg 1929. Der Führer begibt sich zum Kongreß. An diesem Parteitag wurde die Macht des Nationalsozialismus zum ersten Male der Welt klar. Die feindliche Presse tobte. Man begann zu ahnen, daß der Marschtritt der nationalsozialistischen Bataillone nicht mehr zu hemmen war.

Nuremberg 1929. The Führer on the way to the congress meeting. The power of National Socialism will be made clear to the world for the first time at this party conference. The enemy press was in a rage. One began to suspect that the marching steps of the National Socialist battalions could no longer be stopped.

DEUTSCHLAND ERWACHE!
Germany Awake!

THE RISE OF HITLER

Die „Peitsche". Mit großer Empörung haben die feindlichen Blätter gemeldet, daß Hitler immer eine Reitpeitsche bei sich führt. In Wirklichkeit handelt es sich immer um eine Hundepeitsche, die der Führer heute noch zur Erinnerung an die Zeit trägt, da ihm jede Waffe verboten war. Damals war die Peitsche sein einziger Schutz...

The 'whip'. The opposition papers reported with much contempt that Hitler always has a riding whip with him. This is really a dog whip which the Führer only has with him as a reminder of the time during which he was banned from carrying any type of weapon whatsoever. The whip was his only means of protection at the time...

Hitr011

Das Geburtshaus in Braunau am Inn. Hier erblickte Adolf Hitler am 20. April 1889 das Licht der Welt.

His place of birth in Braunau am Inn. This is where Adolf Hitler came into the world on 20 April 1889.

Hitlers Mutter. Diese abgegriffene Photographie trug der Führer während des ganzen Krieges im Brustbeutel über seinem Herzen. Sie war der Talisman seines jahrelangen Kampfes und ist heute noch sein kostbarster Besitz. Hitler sagt, daß er zweimal in seinem Leben geweint habe: am Grabe seiner Mutter und beim Ausbruch der Revolution, als er blind and hilflos von der Zerstörung des Werkes der deutschen Frontsoldaten hörte, dem auch seine Lebensarbeit gegolten hätte...

Hitr014

Hitler´s mother. Hitler had this worn photograph in a neck pouch over his heart throughout the entire war. It was his talisman throughout his fight of many years and is still his most precious possession. Hitler says that he has died twice in his lifetime: beside his mother´s grave and when the revolution broke out, he feeling blind and helpless in the face of the destruction of the work carried out by the German front-line soldiers, this also having been his life´s work...

Hitlers Vater war österreichischer Zollbeamter. Über seinen Vater als Erzieher schreibt Hitler: „… er legte, wenn auch gänzlich unbewußt, die Keime für eine Zukunft, die damals weder er noch ich begriffen hatte."

Hitler´s father was an Austrian customs officer. Hitler wrote the following about the role played by his father in his upbringing: '…without being aware of it, he laid the foundation for a future that neither he nor I have understood'.

Familien=Nachrichten aus Braunau.

Geburten: Am 19. Maria Meirleitner unehel. Kind. — Am 19. Augusta Goßner, Glockengießer-Gehilfenskind. — Am 21. Rudolf Chleborat, Mauteinnehmerskind. Am 21. Theresia Grabmeier, unehel. Kind. Am 20.4.Adolf Hittler, k. k. Zollamts-Offizi alskind.

Hitr013

Sein erstes Bild.

The first photograph showing him.

In der Schule. „Der kleine Rädelsführer" – so bezeichnet sich Hitler selbst in seinem Buch, wenn er über seine ersten Entwicklungsjahre schreibt. Der kleine Adolf Hitler (oberste Reihe, Mitte) mit seinen Klassenkameraden.

At school. 'The small ringleader' – this is how Hitler referred to himself in his book when he wrote about his adolescence. The small Adolf Hitler (in the centre of the top row) with his fellow classmates.

Another class photograph with young Hitler at the back again looking defiant.

...Es war ihm nie vergönnt, diesem Beruf nachzugehen. Aber er wurde zum Baumeister eines neuen Volkes.

...He was prevented from practising this profession but he was to become the architect of a new people.

Courtyard of the Old Residency in Munich. Water colour by Adolf Hitler.

Flower Blossom Study. Water colour by Adolf Hitler.

Perchtoldsdorg Castle and Church. Water colour by Adolf Hitler.

Bridge with Towers. Sketch by Adolf Hitler.

Der Anbruch einer neuen Zeit. Eine vieltausendköpfige Menge singt am 2. August 1914 auf dem Odeonsplatz in München „Die Wacht am Rhein". Mitten im Volk steht einer, den keiner kennt, dessen Namen aber zehn Jahre später ganz Deutschland kennen lernte: Adolf Hitler. „So, wie wohl für jeden Deutschen, begann nun auch für mich die unvergeßlichste und größte Zeit meines irdischen Lebens", schreibt der Führer in seinem berühmten Bekenntnisbuch „Mein Kampf". Das Schicksal hämmerte in seinem Herzen. Am nächsten Tage meldet sich Hitler als Freiwilliger zu einem bayerischen Regiment. Dann zog er in den großen Krieg, den er bis zu seinem bitteren Ende als einer unter viereinhalb Millionen durchkämpfte.

The birth of a new age. A crowd of thousand singing 'The Watch on the Rhine' in Odeon Square, Munich, 2 August 1914. A person is standing in the middle of the crowd who nobody knows but whose name will be in the mouths of all Germans ten years later: Adolf Hitler. 'This was the time when the most unforgettable and greatest time of my life and that of all Germans on earth began', wrote the Führer in his famous confessional book My Fight. Destiny was hammering in his heart. The next day, Hitler volunteered for service with a Bavarian regiment before participating in the Great War that he fought through right to the bitter end, together with four and half million others.

Munich photographer, Heinrich Hoffman, took this photograph of the vast crowd gathered to cheer the declaration of war in 1914. Years later Hitler mentioned that he had been there in Munich on that day. Hoffmann had become Hitler's friend and a meticulous inspection of the photographic prints was made and he was picked out.

An der Front. „Mögen Jahrtausende vergehen, so wird man nie von Heldentum reden und sagen dürfen, ohne des deutschen Heeres des Weltkrieges zu gedenken. Dann wird aus dem Schleier der Vergangenheit heraus die eiserne Front des grauen Stahlhelms sichtbar werden, nicht wankend und nicht weichend, ein Mahnmal der Unsterblichkeit. Solange aber Deutsche leben, werden sie bedenken, daß dies einst Söhne ihres Volkes waren." Den Mann, der viereinhalb Jahre lang unbeirrbar und tapfer seine Pflicht erfüllte für sein deutsche Vaterland, nannte die Regierung eines anderen Deutschland „einen lästigen Auslander". Das erwachende Volk aber weiß, daß Adolf Hitler und Deutschland untrennbare Begriffe sind, während die Welt Hitlers Worte als Äußerungen einer werdenden deutschen Nation betrachtet.

At the front. 'Although centuries might pass, never may the word "heroism" be spoken without having the German World War army in mind. The iron front of the grey steel helmet will then merge from the fogs of the past, not swaying and not yielding, a monument to immortality. As long as there are Germans, they will remember that these were once the sons of these people.' The man who did his duty for his German Fatherland undeviating and valiantly over a period of four and half years was once referred to as 'a troublesome foreigner' by the Government of another Germany. The awaking people know however that Adolf Hitler and Germany are inseparable entities, whereas Hitler´s words are to be looked upon as statements of a German nation in the making

Hitler's dog tags: Left, Bavarian Reserve Infantry Regiment 13, 3.Companie, number 718.
Right: Bavarian Reserve Infantry Regiment 16, 1.Companie, number 148.

Der Soldat. „Ich war eine Nummer im Weltkrieg wie Millionen andere auch." Die „Kapelle Krach" versuchte mit Erfolg Stimmung und Fröhlichkeit zu schaffen.

The soldier. 'During the World War, I was just a number like millions of others were.' The 'Kapelle Krach' or the Racket Band tried to create a good mood and happiness and that with success.

Hitler (sitzend, außen rechts) mit seinen Feldkameraden vom Bayerischen Reserve-Infanterie-Regiment 16

Hitler (seated, far right) with his field comrades from the Bavarian Reserve Infantry Regiment No. 16.

Ein anderes Erinnerungsbild aus der Kriegszeit. Links vorn: Adolf Hitler

Another souvenir picture from the war- Front left: Adolf Hitler

Verwundet. Nach einer Granatsplitterverletzung im Jahre 1916 am linken Oberschenkel mußte der Führer für kurze Zeit die Front verlassen. Am 13. Oktober 1918 erhielt er seine schwerste Verwundung durch Gelbkreuzgas an der Südfront von Ypern.
Erblindet erlebte er im Lazarett Pasewalk in Pommern die Revolution. Als er sehend geworden war, stand ihm sein Lebensziel vor Augen: Vernichtung der marxistischen Verräter.

Wounded. The Führer had to leave the front briefly in 1916 after being injured by a shrapnel in his left thigh. He suffered his worst wound on 13 October 1918, when he suffered poisoning by yellow-cross gas on the southern front of Ypres.
He experienced the revolution when he was blind in a military hospital in Pasewalk, Pomerania. When he regained his sight, he had his goal in life in front of him: the destruction of the Marxist traitors.

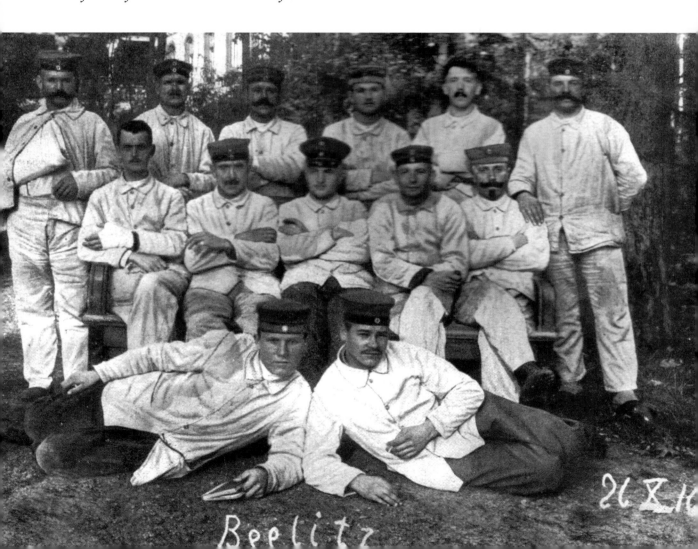

Beelitz

26 X 16

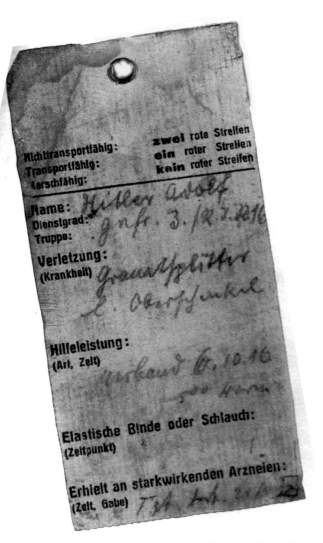

Der Berliner Polizeipräsident Grzesinski nannte ihn „Deserteur"! Eine Seite aus dem Militärpaß Adolf Hitlers mit Angabe der ihm wegen hervorragender Tapferkeit verliehenen Auszeichnungen.

The Berlin Police Commissioner, Grzesinski, referred to him as a 'Deserter'! A page from Adolf Hitler´s service record including information on the honours that had been conferred on him for excellent valour.

Albert Karl Wilhelm Grzesinski.

Datum		zu den Personal-Notizen.
		(Einberufungen, Führung, Strafen ꝛc.)

Kgl. Res. Inf. Rgt. No. 16
3. Komp. 7.
3.
19

Gefechte:

Vorm. v. 3. 17 bis 15. 10. d. bei
der 3. Durchg. Bayer. Res. Inf. Rgt.
no. 16.

den 15. 10. 18 bei Neulager gestürzt

27. 9. 17 E. K. 2. Klasse
voz Jahre

9. d. A. Regts. Diplom
f. hervorragende Tapfer-
keit während des Ein-
sagzes an Frankreich

4. 8. 18 Sachs. Krieg I. Klasse

18. 8. 18 Königl. Abz. f. Soldaten

25. 8. 18 E. K. 2. Klasse

Lösung:

Strafen:

Als der Kampf begann... Aufnahme des Führers aus dem Jahr 1921, als Hitler anfing, in immer größer werdenden Versammlungen das deutsche Volk zum Widerstand aufzurufen.

When the fight started... Photographs of the Führer from 1921 when he started speaking before a constantly increasing number of crowds, urging the German people to revolt.

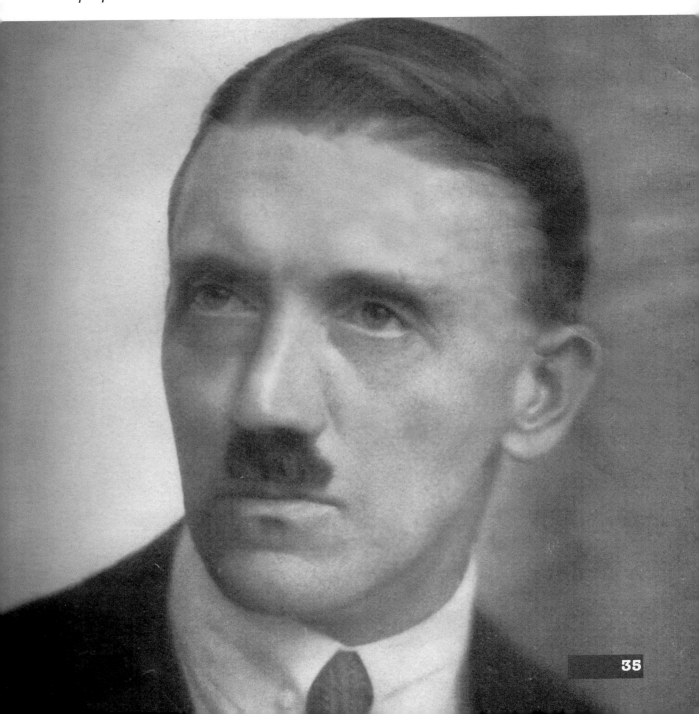

Die erste Aufnahme des Führers bei Beginn seiner politischen Tätigkeit: Fahnenweihe auf dem Marsfeld München 1923

The first photograph of the Führer taken at the beginning of his political career: the flag ordination on the Marsfeld parade ground in Munich 1923.

Facing up to the German Communists for the first time with military weapons, Hitler oversees a machine gun team, 1 May 1923.

Endless campaining for power: Hitler during an election campaign strikes poses for the people and the cameras. He chooses to appear confident and in control — a man to whom the voters can entrust their future.

So war es 1922! Windjacken, Skimützen, derbe Stöcke. Aus diesen primitiven Anfängen heraus entwickelte sich die gewaltige Organisation der Nationalsozialistischen SA. Eine Idee begann Gestalt zu werden, die Marschkolonnen des Nationalsozialismus setzten sich in Bewegung.

That was what it was like in 1922! Windcheaters, ski caps, roughly hewn sticks. The gigantic national socialist SA developed from these primitive beginnings. An idea started to take form and the marching columns of national socialism started to move.

Auch der Führer trug damals den SA.-Stock…

The Führer also held the SA stick at the time…

1923 waren es schon Tausende und Abertausende, die sich dem Führer zur Freiheit verschworen hatten. Feiger Verrat versuchte an jenem dunklen 9. November die junge Bewegung zu vernichten. Aber mächtiger denn je erhob sie sich.

In 1923, many thousand conspired to restrict the Führer´s freedom. Cowardly treachery attempted to destroy the new movement on that dark 9th of November but it rose again, stronger than ever.

HIT36 Some of the very first Nazis: Hitler with Schaub, Schreck and Schneider.

November 9, 1923 marks the date of Hitler's attempted Bierkellerputsch (beer hall putsch) in Munich, his failed attempt to overthrow the Weimar Republic (in which four Bavarian policemen and a bystander were killed, in addition to 16 'Putschisten')

HIT55 Barricades erected and manned by the Nazis in front of the War Ministry 9 November 1923. Around 3,000 people joined Hitler at that time and the push for power failed.

A large crowd gathers in front of the Rathaus to hear the exhortations of Julius Streicher during the Beer Hall Putsch.

Leaders of the Beer Hall Putsch, 1923, awaiting trial (left to right): Heinz Pernet, Friedrich Weber, Wilhelm Frick, Hermann Kriebel, Erich Ludendorff, Adolf Hitler, Wilhelm Brückner, Ernst Röhm, Robert Heinrich Wagner.

A camera smuggled into the court room was used to take this photograph of the proceedings when the trial of the leaders of the failed coup took place in 1924.

Landsberg Prison located in the town of Landsberg am Lech in the southwest of the German state of Bavaria, about 40 miles west of Munich. Hitler was confined here for nine months of a five year sentence.

Der Führer in seiner Zelle in der Landsberger Festung, wo er 1923 und 1924 gefangen gehalten wurde

The Führer in his cell in Landsberg Fortress, where he was held prisoner in 1923 and 1924

The conditions of Hitler's incarceration in Landsberg Prison were comfortable, and he used his time there to write Mein Kampf. Hitler is pictured in his cell Adolf Hitler, Rudolf Hess, Kriebel, J. Fobke and Dr Friedrich Weber. Date, February 1924.

Visitors could come and go as they pleased and Hitler was able to formulate ideas for his book *Mein Kampf* (My Struggle).

Hitler began dictating the book to his deputy, Rudolf Hess, from his prison cell. Although Hitler received many visitors initially, he soon devoted himself entirely to the book. As he continued, Hitler realized that it would have to be a two-volume work, with the first volume scheduled for release in early 1925.

The governor of Landsberg noted at the time that Hitler hoped the book would run into many editions, thus enabling him to fulfill his financial obligations and to defray the expenses incurred at the time of his trial.

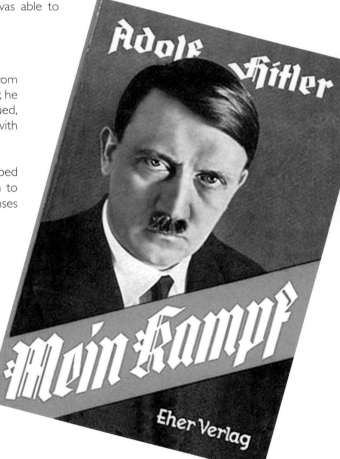

Hitler leaves Landsberg prison and a snapshot is taken by his friend, Heinrich Hoffmann,

Nach dreistündiger Rede schreitet der Führer erschöpft durch das Spalier der SA- und SS-Kameraden, umbraust von dem Jubel der Tausende, die durch ihn einen neuen Glauben und eine neue Hoffnung gewonnen haben.

After having held a three-hour talk, the Führer walks exhausted through the guard of honour provided by the SA and SS comrades, surrounded by the roaring jubilation of the thousands that have gained new faith and new hope through him.

'Martyrs' of the Munich Putsch. It reads AND YOU HAVE WON.

THESE MEN FELL ON November 9, 1923 BEFORE FELDHERRNHALLE AND IN THE COURTYARD OF THE WAR DEPARTMENT IN THE LOYAL HOPE FOR THE RESURRECTION OF YOUR PEOPLE.

Der Redner. Die Nationalsozialistische Deutsche Arbeiterpartei wurde groß durch ihre Massenpropaganda. Noch heute ist Adolf Hitler nicht nur der Führer, sondern auch der erste Propagandist seiner Bewegung. Wie Hammerschläge fallen seine Worte in die Herzen der Zehntausende, die ihm zuhören: „Man bettelt nicht für ein Recht, für ein Recht kämpft man"

The speaker. The National Socialist German Workers Party expanded due to its mass propaganda. It is still the case today that Adolf Hitler is not only the Führer, but also the first propagandist of his movement. His words are driven into the hearts of the tens of the thousand that listen to him. 'One does not beg for a right, one fights for a right.'

In the year following his release, 1925, Hitler re-founded and reorganized the Nazi Party, with himself as its undisputed Leader.

Die Hände des Führers gestalten plastisch seine Rede. Eine Aufnahme bannte Hitlers Hände, als er von der Einheit von nationalsozialistischer uns sozialistischer Idee sprach.

The Führer's hands sculpture his talk vividly. A photograph shows Hitler's hands when he is talking about the unity of national socialist and socialist ideas.

Die Antwort an das System. Ihr sagt: „Wir bleiben um jeden Preis" – ich sage: „Wir schlagen euch auf alle Fälle"

The reply to the system. You say: 'We shall stay whatever happens' – I say: 'We shall beat you whatever happens.'

HIT42 Hitler surrounded by his stormtroopers.

„… 13 Jahre habe ich in Deutschland gepredigt, unzählige Millionen kennen unser Programm, nur ein Mann hat von alledem nichts erfahren: der Herr Reichsinnenminister Groener"

"…I have been preaching in Germany for 13 years, millions know our manifesto, only one man claims that he has never heard of it: the Reich Minister of the Interior Herr Groener!"

Karl Eduard Wilhelm Groener.
Reich Minister of the Interior.

His hand movements and facial expressions were carefully staged to achieve the best possible effect on his spell-bound audience.

Hitler spricht! Gespannteste Aufmerksamkeit, Glaube, Treue – im Antlitz seiner Kämpfer spiegelt sich das Erlebnis seiner Rede.

Hitler is speaking! Excited attention, belief, loyalty – the effect of his address is mirrored in the faces of his fighters.

„Heil Hitler", der Ruf der Jugend, die seinen Namen trägt

'Heil Hitler', the call of the youth that bears his name.

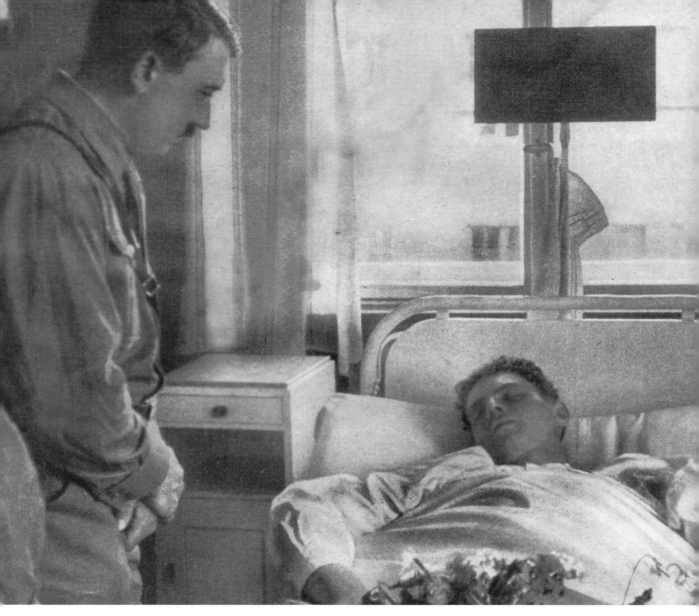

Ein Toter ruft zur Tat. Hitler am Totenbett eines SS-Kamaraden. Als der Führer an das Lager des sterbenden trat, bäumte sich dieser noch einmal auf und reckte mit einem letzten „Heil Hitler" seinem Führer den Arm entgegen. Wieder war ein tapferer Nationalsozialist für Adolf Hitler in den Tod gegangen. „Kam´raden, die Rotfront und Reaktion erschossen, marschier´n im Geist in unsren Reihen mit"

A dying man calls to action. Hitler beside the deathbed of an SS comrade. When the Führer came to the bedside of the dying man, he reared up and stretched his arm towards the Führer with a last 'Heil Hitler'. Another brave national socialist has died for Adolf Hitler. 'Comrades shot by the Red Front and the result of those shot is that they march in spirit in our ranks alongside us.'

German Communists – 'The Red Front' enemy of Hitler's Nazi Party.

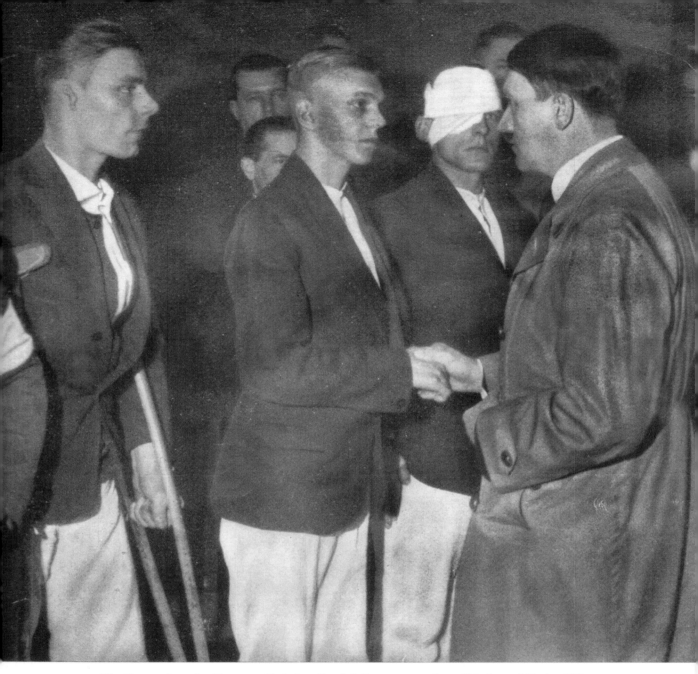

Die Treuesten der Treuen. Bei den Besichtigungen seiner SA, begrüßt der Führer stets die Verwundeten zuerst und dankt Ihnen für ihren heldenhaften Einsatz. Generalappell der Berliner SA im Sportpalast

The most devoted of his loyal followers. When inspecting his SA, the Führer always meets the wounded first and thanks them for their heroism. General roll call of the Berlin SA in Sportpalast.

HIT43 Hitler grasps the Blütfahne (Blood Flag) at a Party Rally at Nuremberg in 1929. It was supposedly stained with the blood of the Nazis who lost their lives in the failed Munich putsch in 1923.

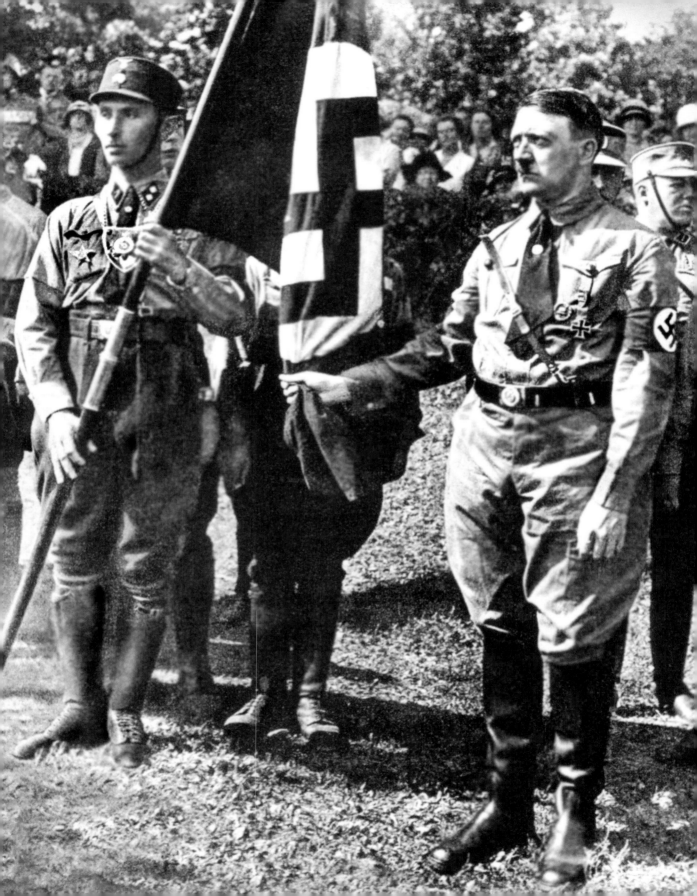

Ernst Julius Günther Röhm in conversation with Hitler. The former German officer in the Bavarian Army became an early Nazi leader, he was a co-founder of the Nazi Party militia, the Sturmabteilung, (Storm Battalion; SA), and became its commander. Röhm was arrested by Hitler, who viewed him as a rival, and was executed at Stadelheim prison, Munich, in July 1934.

Harzburg. Der Führer der national Opposition begrüßt eine Abteilung seiner SS.

Harzburg. The Leader of the national opposition takes the salute of a division of his SS.

Reichstagswahl 1930. Am 14. September schnellte die Zahl der nationalsozialistischen Abgeordneten im deutschen Reichstag von 12 auf 107 empor. Nach der Verkündung des Wahlergebnisses steht Adolf Hitler lächelnd im Jubel seiner Anhänger. (Neben dem Führer: sein langjähriger Mitarbeiter, Max Amann, Direktor des Zentralverlages der NSDAP).

Reichstag election 1930. On 14 September, the number of National Socialist members of the Reichstag shot up from 12 to 107. Adolf Hitler being acclaimed by his supporters after the election results had been announced. (Next to the Führer: Max Amann, Director of the central NSDAP publishing house).

Der Führer mit Pg. Schreck
The Führer with Pg. Schreck

Hitler presides over an informal meeting of the NSDAP at the Hofbräuhaussaal, 1932.

For the camera Hitler reads the front page of the *Völkischer Beobachter* (National Observer) newspaper of the NSDAP or Nazi Party, from 1920.

Wenn im Winter die Wege für den Kraftwagen unbefahrbar werden, fährt der Führer die weiten Strecken mit der Eisenbahn. Außer diesen wenigen Wochen fährt Hitler immer mit seinem Kraftwagen, einem großen Mercedes-Benz Wagen, der ihm große Sicherheit verbürgt und von der Zeit unabhängig macht.

When the roads are impassible for the car in winter, the Führer travels long distances by train. With the exception of these few weeks, Hitler always uses his car, a large Mercedes-Benz, which provides him with a great amount of safety and enables him to be more flexible in terms of time.

Auch hier läßt ihm Photo-Hoffmann keine Ruhe.

The photographer Hoffmann also does not even leave him alone here.

Der Hundeliebhaber. In seinem Berghaus hat der Führer eine Zucht schönster Schäferhunde. Er liebt sie fast so sehr wie sie ihn.

The dog lover. The Führer has a breed of the most beautiful Alsatians in his house in the mountains. He loves them almost as much as they do him.

Als böse Menschen ihn in seinem Innersten treffen wollten, vergifteten sie seinen Lieblingshund. So kämpft die Gemeinheit gegen einen guten Menschen.

When evil people wanted to hurt him down to the very heart they poisoned his favourite dog. This is how meanness fights against good people.

Haus Wachenfeld, 'Berghof' Obersalzberg, Berchtesgaden. before the house was renovated. It was bought by Hitler in 1933 and serious remodelling was undertaken.

Erholung. Abgeschieden von Lärm und Unruhe der Städte ruht hier der Führer auf den großen Wiesen in der Nähe seines Häuschens von den Strapazen des Kampfes aus. Dabei liest er dann die gegnerischen Zeitungen und freut sich über die Märchen, die sie über ihn verbreiten: Sektgelage, jüdische Freundinnen, Luxusvilla, französische Gelder ...

Relaxation. The Führer resting in a meadow close to his house, away from the noise and unrest of the city and his struggle. He then likes to read the opposing newspapers and has pleasure at the reports on the fairy-tales they tell about him: sparkling wine binges, Jewish girlfriends, a luxury villa, French money ...

Die Bergwiese bei seinem „Häus´l", ein idyllischer Hang zur erholung und Ruhe

The mountain meadow close to his small house, an idyllic hillside for rest and relaxation

In der „Kurz'n".

In the 'shorts'.

Hitler decided that for photographs to appear with him wearing shorts would not be dignified and he stopped publication of such images.

In den geliebten Bergen. Von Zeit zu Zeit sucht der Führer für Stunden oder kurze Tage seine „Villa" in den bayrischen Bergen auf, eine kleines Holzhaus, das seine Schwester gepachtet hat. Dort findet er die innere Sammlung und Kraft zu neuer Arbeit.

In his beloved mountains. The Führer goes to his 'villa' now and again. This is a small wooden cabin that his sister has rented in the Bavarian mountains. This is where he finds the spiritual repose and the strength he needs to start new work.

Sein Lieblingsplatz am Hochlenzer. Hier weilte auch Dietrich Eckart während seiner Verbannung

His favourite place on Hochlenzer in Berchtesgarten. This is where Dietrich Eckart also stayed during his exile.

Dietrich Eckart participated in the failed Beer Hall Putsch. He was arrested and placed in Landsberg Prison along with Hitler and other party officials, but was released due to illness. He died of a heart attack in Berchtesgaden 26 December 1923.

Bei der Schwester. Die Zeitungslektüre ergibt: Lügen und immer wieder Lügen, aber die Wahrheit ist nicht aufzuhalten. Die Glaube an den Führer ist größer als die Macht der Presse.

With his sister. A perusal of the newspaper produced the same results as always: lies and even more lies, but the truth cannot be stopped. The belief in the Führer is greater than the power of the press.

Hitler's niece, Geli Raubal, was his ward and one great love. Hitler was domineering and possessive of Raubal and did not allow her to freely associate with friends. On 18 September 1931 she shot herself in Hitler's Munich apartment with his Walther pistol. She was 23-years-old at the time. Her half uncle was heart-broken and immersed himself in his political life.

Hitler's car approaching the town of Ellingen during his political campaigning.

Das alte Stadttor von Elligen
The old city gate of Ellingen.

Hitler checks his map during an election tour.

Begegnung auf der Landstraße. Auf seinen Reisen durch die deutschen Gaue trifft der Führer überall Mitkämpfer.

Encounter on a country road. The Führer meets his fellow-combatants everywhere during his journeys through the German Gaus or military districts.

Heil Hitler! Den Abfahrenden Wagen umdrängen die begeisterten Parteigenossen.

Heil Hitler! The enthralled party comrades surround the departing car.

Begegnung auf der Landstraße. Wandernde Nationalsozialisten erkennen ihn unterwegs, bekommen von ihm seinen Namenszug.

Encounter on a country road. Hiking National Socialists recognise him on the road and he gives them his autograph.

Überall Mitkämpfer! Keine Fahrt ohne Zusammentreffen mit Kameraden, die ihm unterwegs zuwinken, ihm von ihren Kampf erzählen. Ein fester Händedruck und sie fahren weiter: der unbekannte SA-Mann und sein geliebter Führer, beide dienende am gemeinsamen Werk.

Fellow-combatants everywhere! No journey without meeting comrades, who wave at him and tell him about their fight. A firm handshake and they continue on their way: the unidentified SA man and his popular Führer, both serving a common cause.

Während der kurzen Fahrtunterbrechungen liest der Führer die Post.

The Führer reads the mail during a short break in the journey.

Rast am Wege. In den Städten findet der Führer keine Ruhe. Überall erkannt, ist es ihm unmöglich, dort eine stille Stunde zu verleben. So verzehrt er das einfache Mittagsmahl an irgendeinem abgelegenen Waldrand. Rechts: Hermann Esser.

A break en route. The Führer is unable to find any rest in the cities. He is recognised everywhere, making it impossible to spend a restful hour there so he enjoys his simple lunch at the remote edge of an unknown forest. On the right: Hermann Esser.

Hermann Esser was an early member of the Nazi party, who joined in 1920 with Adolf Hitler. A journalist, Esser was the editor of the Nazi paper, Völkischer Beobachter.

Ein Anspruchsloser. In wenigen Stunden werden ihm Zehntausende zujubeln...

An unpretentious man. Tens of thousands will be acclaiming him just a few hours later...

Der Sohn des Volkes. Keinem anderen in Deutschland gilt so die Liebe des deutschen Arbeiters wie Adolf Hitler. Wo er auch immer ist, bricht diese Liebe spontan hervor. Ob es Tausende sind, die ihm zujubeln, oder ob ein Einzelner ihm die Hand drückt, sie alle sehen in ihm den Befreier und danken ihm mit dem Leuchten ihrer Augen

The son of the people. Nobody in Germany was so loved by the German worker as Adolf Hitler. This love breaks out of them spontaneously when they see him. No matter whether it is the thousand that acclaim him, or the individual that shakes his hand, they all look on him as their rescuer and thank him with shining eyes.

Bei Freunden. Große Feste liebt der Führer nicht. Im Kreise seiner Freunde sucht er Entspannung von schwerer Arbeit. Bei seinem Gauführer Röver in Oldenburg.

Together with friends. The Führer does not like large parties. He likes to relax from hard work with friends. Together with his Gauleiter Röver in Oldenberg.

Carl Georg Röver.
Gauleiter of Oldenberg.

A visit to a factory belonging to a financial contributor of the NSDAP.

Die führer der Industrie. Industrie-Club Düsseldorf.

The industrial leaders. Dusseldorf Industry Club.

This photograph seems to have frozen a dramatic moment in time: the speaker's words appear to have angered Herman Göring, who clearly has clenched his fist and is fixing the Führer with a hard stare. Hitler is looking quizzically at the man on the right, who may well be an industrial leader. Perhaps Hitler is about to ask 'Am I hearing this right?'

Er ist in der Lage, um die arbeitenden Menschen zu gewinnen.

He is able to attract the working man.

Ist Hitler ein Ketzer? Der Führer als Trauzeuge bei der Hochzeit seines Festungskamerades und jetzigen ständigen treuen Begleiters Schaub.

Is Hitler a heretic? The Führer as witness at the wedding of his fortress comrade and now permanent loyal companion Schaub.

Julius Schaub.

Eine photographische Zufälligkeit wird zum Symbol. Adolf Hitler, der angebliche „Ketzer", beim Verlassen der Marinekirche in Wilhelmshaven.

A photographic coincidence is turned into a symbol. Adolf Hitler, who some claim to be a 'heretic', leaving the navy church in Wilhelmshaven.

HIT44 Ludwig Müller leader of the German Faith Movement shakes hands with Hitler at the Nuremberg Rally 1934.

HIT45 Church leader Müller salutes at a Nazi gathering.

HIT49Roman Catholic Church leaders show their approval and 'Heil Hitler'.

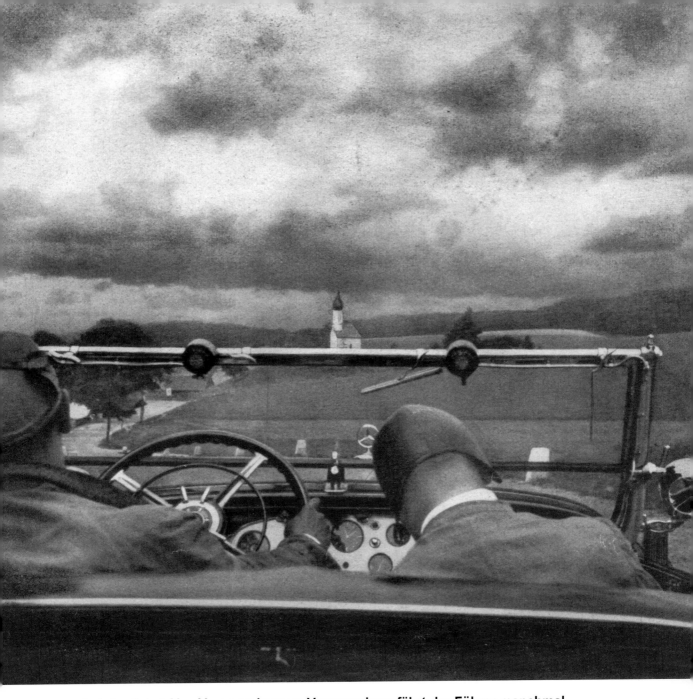

Auf der Fahrt. Von Versammlung zu Versammlung fährt der Führer manchmal Nächte hindurch. Während Kilometer auf Kilometer überwunden wird, schläft er dann erschöpft von den Anstrengungen einer Riesenkundgebung

On the road. At times, the Führer drives through the night from conference to conference. He then sleeps, exhausted from the efforts of an enormous rally while the car eats up the road kilometre for kilometre.

Das letzte Porträt des Führers vor der Reichspräsidentenwahl.

The last portrait of the Führer before the Reichspresident election.

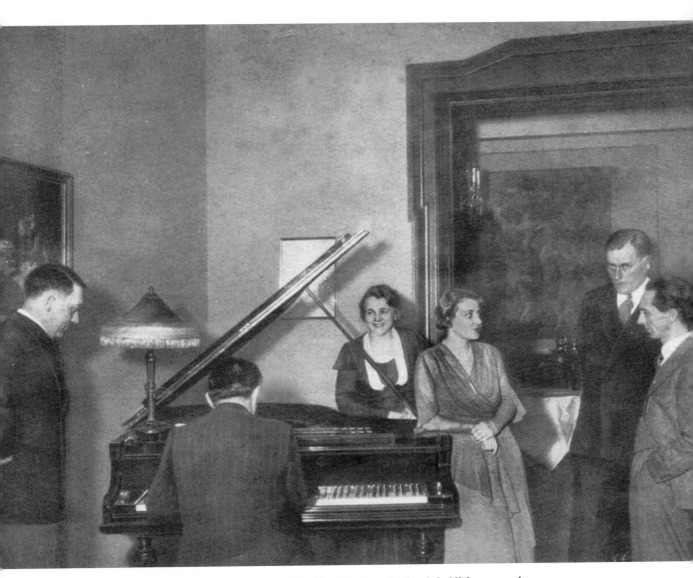

Im Hause des Berliner Gauleiters Dr. Goebbels erholt sich Hitler von den Anstrengungen der Berliner Verhandlungen

Hitler relaxes from the exertions of the Berlin negotiations at the house of the Berlin Gauleiter, Dr. Goebbels.

On the road. Often Hitler drove through the night from conference to party rally as he sought to win the hearts of the German people.

Auch die Jüngsten wollen ihr Hitlerbild haben.

Even the youngest want to have a photo of Hitler.

Das ganze Deutschland ist seine Heimat! An der Nordsee …

All of Germany is his home! On the North Sea coast…

… und am Bodensee. Oft durchmißt er in wenigen Tagen sein Vaterland von Nord nach Süd, von Ost nach West.

… and at Lake Constance. He often crosses his Fatherland from north to south, from east to west in just a few days.

Am Landungssteg. Kurze Rast auf der Reise nach Ostpreußen.

On the jetty. A short break on the way to East Prussia.

Abfahrt. Hitler verabschiedet sich vom Führer der ostpreußischen SA, Gruppenführer Litzmann, Sohn des berühmten Generals

Departure. Hitler takes leave of the Commander of the East Prussian SA, Group Commander Litzmann, the son of the famous general.

Karl-Siegmund Litzmann.

Auf der Rückfahrt von Ostpreußen. „Nicht West- und nicht Ostorientierung darf das künftige Ziel unserer Außenpolitik sein, sondern Ostpolitik im Sinne der Erwerbung der notwendigen Scholle für unser deutsches Volk"

On the return journey from East Prussia. 'The future objective of our foreign policy should not be a west or an east orientation, but an east policy in the sense of acquiring the space on earth that our German people needs.'

An der Nordsee beobachtet der Führer die Manöver der Reichsmarine. „Die Unzertrennlichen", der Führer, sein Privatsekretär Heß und sein Fahrer Schreck.

The Führer observes the Reich Navy manoeuvring in the North Sea. 'The inseparables', the Führer, his private secretary Hess and his driver Schreck.

Die Lebenshaltung Adolf Hitlers ist denkbar einfach. Er trinkt nie ein Tropfen Alkohol und er ist Nichtraucher

Adolf Hitler´s approach to life is quite simple: he never drinks a drop of alcohol and he does not smoke.

Besuch in Thüringen. Hinter dem Führer: sein ständiger Begleiter Julius Schaub, der mit ihm auf der Festung war

Visit to Thuringia. Behind the Führer: his permanent companion Julius Schaub who was with him in Landsberg Prison.

Begrüßung in Harzburg.

Welcome in Harzburg.

Hitler mit den Söhnen eines alten Parteigenossen.

Hitler with the sons of an old party comrade.

Wer die Zukunft hat, der hat die Jugend!

He who has the future, has the youth!

Die Jugend liebt ihn. Überall drängen sich Kinder an ihn heran, um ihm Blumen zu bringen.

The youth love him. Children try to get close to him everywhere so that they can give him flowers.

In einem kleinen Städtchen des bayrischen Allgäu bringt ihm die Jugend ihren Blumengruß

The youths in a small town in Bavarian Allgäu bring him flowers as a welcome.

Hitler-Jugend. Auch die Jüngsten sind seine Kämpfer ...

Hitler Youth. Even the youngest fight for him...

Der Schöpfer des Braunen Hauses.
The creator of the Brown House.

„Es geschieht nichts in dieser Bewegung ohne meine Willen." Der Führer in seinem Arbeitszimmer im Braunen Haus. Von hier aus leitet er die Riesenorganisation der NSDAP.

'Nothing happens in this movement without my knowledge.' The Führer in his study in the Brown House. From here he steers the gigantic NSDAP organization.

Der Führer bei einem Besuch in der Wohnung des Gruppenführers Lutze in Hannover.

The Führer during a visit to the flat of Group Commander Lutze in Hanover.

Gruppenführer Viktor Lutze, an officer in the SA. His participation at the 'Night of the Long Knives' was significant, due to the fact that he was the one to inform Adolf Hitler about Ernst Röhm's anti-regime activities. After the purge he was the new leader of the SA until his death in a car accident in 1943.

Der Führer mit Reichspressechef Dr. Dietrich.

The Führer with Chief Press Officer Dr. Dietrich.

Otto Dietrich was appointed Press Chief of the NSDAP in 1931 and the following year joined the SS. By 1941 he had risen to the rank of SS-*Obergruppenführer.*

Täglich überwachte Adolf Hitler den Bau des Braunen Hauses in Begleitung seines Mitarbeiters und Freundes Franz Schwarz, des Reichsschatzmeisters der Bewegung.

Adolf Hitler supervised the construction of the Brown House every day, accompanied by his employee and friend Franz Schwarz, the Reich Minister of the Movement.

Franz Xaver Schwarz a politician who served as Reichsschatzmeister (National Treasurer) of the Nazi Party (NSDAP) during most of the Party's existence.

Ende des Jahres 1921 bezieht die NSDAP ein neues Geschäftslokal in der Corneliusstraße 12 zu München.

The NSDAP moved into new offices at Corneliusstraße 12 in Munich at the end of 1921.

10 Jahre Später: Das Braune Haus. Zum ersten Male erhält die Bewegung einen machtvollen Ausdruck ihres Wollens durch die Schaffung des Nationalsozialistischen Parteiheims, das zu einem Wahrzeichen Münchens geworden ist. Darüber hinaus ist das Braune Haus für alle Nationalsozialisten das Symbol ihrer einheitlichen Geschlossenheit.

Ten years later: the Brown House. The movement is presented with a powerful expression of its will with the erection of the National Socialist Party offices, which has become a Munich landmark. Not only that: the Brown House has become that symbol of close unity for all National Socialists.

Das Braune Haus in München ist das Ziel der SA aus allen Gauen Deutschlands. Wie leuchten ihre Augen, wenn der Führer in ihrer Nähe weilt!

The Brown House in Munich is the destination for the SA from all areas in Germany. How their eyes light up when the Führer is close to them!

Beim Bau des Hitler-Hauses in Nürnberg. Der fränkische Parteiführer Julius Streicher und Hitler bei einer Besprechung.

During the construction of the Hitler House in Nuremberg. The Franconian Party Leader Julius Streicher and Hitler during a discussion.

Bei Professor Troost, dem Architekten des Braunen Hauses.

Together with Professor Troost, the architect of the Brown House.

Seine große Natursehnsucht kann Hitler nur selten befriedigen. Sein Leben heißt Kampf und Arbeit.

Hitler can seldom fulfill his passion for nature. His life means conflict and work.

Market Square
Berchtesgarten.

Members of the Hitler Youth gathered on the Obersalzberg pack the road leading past Haus Wachenfeld.

Autographs and photographs for the Hitler Youth members.

Among the crowd is a little girl who tells him that her birthday is on the same day as the Führer's, 20 April. Hitler escorts little Bernile Nienau up to Haus Wachenfeld later the Berghof. She and her mother became regular visitors to Hitler's home until Martin Bormann discovered she was not of pure Aryan descent.

Autographs and handshakes for some of the fortunate children gathered at Haus Wachenfeld.

A little visitor receives a gift from Hitler. This photograph is taken on the terrace of Haus Wachenfeld and the girl may belong to a family of a Party member.

Even toddlers were photographed with the Führer. Although this little girl does not appear to know what it is all about.

The Führer with his dog Blondi in the conservatory at Haus Wachenfeld. The dog was a gift from Martin Bormann.

It has been said that Hitler's love of children was genuine enough. Here two little girls seem absorbed in their world and the Führer looks on amused.

A portrait of Hitler in SA uniform. After this photograph was taken he never wore it again.

A much preferred image for the world's press.

Two generations explain why they back the Führer on this postcard.

'All Germans listen to the Führer' is the slogan.

In the 1932 elections a radio broadcast by Hitler reached millions of Germans in their homes.

Hitler shares a joke with his pilot and bodyguard as he leaves for Berlin from Münich in March 1933.

Hitler leaving a meeting with President von Hindenburg in August 1932.

Paul von Hindenburg Prussian-German field marshal, statesman, and politician. He served as the second President of Germany from 1925 to 1934.

Hitler, von Hindenburg and Göring at the Battle of Tannenberg Memorial and observance in August 1933.

President von Hindenburg and his Chancellor. The delight on Hitler's face is obvious as he progresses towards absolute power.

Top hat and tails for this occasion at Potsdam on 21 March 1933. Crown Prince Wilhelm, the Kaiser's son, discusses a matter with Hitler with Göring looking at the camera.

Hitler acknowledges the cheering crowd gathered outside the Reichschancellery the night he took power, 30 January 1933.

Hitler nimmt starken Anteil an der deutschen Marine und läßt keine Gelegenheit vorübergehen, um sich über ihre Entwicklungsmöglichkeiten unterrichten zu können.

Hitler shows great interest in the German navy and does not miss any opportunity to obtain information on its development.

Hitler tries yet another pose for the camera; another image destined for eager consumption by the adoring masses.

Hitler, der Architekt, zeigt den SA-Männern in Paulinzella in Thüringen einen alten Klostergang. In Paulinenzella befindet sich das Heim der Thüringer SA.

Hitler the architect, shows the SA men in Paulinzella, Thuringia old cloisters. Paulinzella is the home of the Thuringian SA.

Der Führer läßt sich über die Lage der norddeutschen Landwirtschaft unterricht-en. Da sein Vater nach Abschluß seiner Amtszeit einen kleinen Bauernhof erwor-ben hatte, ist Hitler von Kindheit auf in diesem Berufe heimisch

The Führer obtains information on the agricultural situation in North Germany. Hitler has been at home in this profession since he was a child as his father purchased a small farm when he retired.

Der Führer am Flugzeug seines Privatsekretärs Heß. Auch für das Flugwesen zeigt Adolf Hitler größtes Interesse

The Führer next to the aircraft belonging to his private secretary Hess. Adolf Hitler is also greatly interested in aviation.

… Besichtigung einer Station zur Rettung Schiffbrüchiger: Hitlers Interesse für Schiffahrt ist unbegrenzt

… visiting a lifeboat station. Hitler´s maritime interest knows no bounds.

Im Nietzsche-Archiv in Weimar. Der Führer an der Büste des deutschen Philosophen, dessen Ideen zwei große Volksbewegungen befruchteten: die nationalsozialistische Deutschlands und die faschistische Italiens.

In the Nietzsche Archive in Weimar. The Führer looking at the bust of the German philosopher, whose ideas stimulated two great grassroots movements: the national socialist in German and the fascist in Italy.

Eingebürgert! Der Führer empfängt in seinem Arbeitszimmer im Hotel Kaiserhof die Mitteilung von seiner Ernennung zum braunschweigischen Regierungsrat. Ein jahrelanger Frevel wird damit gesühnt: der Frontsoldat Hitler wird endlich deutscher Staatsbürger

Naturalised! The Führer, in his study in the Kaiserhof Hotel, receives the news that he has been appointed a Brunswick councillor. An injustice of many years standing has been put right: the German soldier, Hitler, is now finally a German citizen.

An informal group at Haus Wachenfeld. Hitler has just become Chancellor of Germany.

An impression of good fellowship is conveyed in this picture taken in front of the Reich chancellery during the British Legion's visit to Germany in July 1935.

Royal British Legion officials Major Featherstone-Godley and Colonel Crosfield in a discussion at the Reich Reich chancellery in Berlin, July 1935.

An unusual photograph of the Berghof taken from a light aircraft. It shows the conservatory and terrace built over the garage. The roofline of Haus Wachenfeld can be seen behind the new construction. It appears that the massive picture window is still being fitted.

Hitler takes up position at the bottom of the drive to greet visitors to the Berghof.

The Duke and Duchess of Windsor stand for a group photograph before their departure following a state visit in October 1937. The shot is taken on the steps of the Berghof.

The Führer greets Lloyd George at the Burghof. in March 1936.

Hitler welcomes the British Prime Minister, Neville Chamberlain, who is greeted on the steps of the Berghof by Hitler. He was on a mission to avoid war over German demands concerning territory of Sudetenland in Czechoslovakia.

The Duke and Duchess of Windsor leaving the Berghof after their visit to Obersalzberg in 1937.

The Munich Conference: Prime Minister Neville Chamberlain; French Premier Daladier; Hitler; Benito Mussolini; Count Ciano (Italian Foreign Minister and Mussolini's son-in-law).

The Rise of Hitler to world prominence had occured certainly by 1938, when the British and French prime ministers came to his table to give in to the Führer of Germany's demands. The dictator of Italy, Mussolini, was also present at the meeting, giving his support to his fellow despot.

Hitler on the steps of the Berghof with the other woman in his life (see page 89). Eva Braun was a photographer working for Heinrich Hoffman when she met Hitler. She was a key figure within Hitler's inner social circle, but did not attend public events with him until the Summer of 1944. As Germany's total defeat neared she went to Berlin to be by his side in the heavily reinforced underground bunker beneath the Reich Chancellery. As Soviet troops fought their way towards the Führerbunker she and Hitler were married 29 April 1945; she was 33 and he was 56. Less than 40 hours after their marriage, they committed suicide together.